AF265146

RANDOM

OTHER BOOKS BY ADAM WALLACE

Better Out Than In

Better Out Than In Number Twos

Rhymes With Art — Learn Cartooning the Fun Way

Accidentally Awesome

Jamie Brown is ~~NOT~~ Rich

RANDOM

ADAM WALLACE

Random

Published by Classic Author and Publishing Services Pty Ltd

© 2015 JoJo Publishing Imprint

This edition published in the year of the werewolf 2015
Second reprint 2015

National Library of Australia
Cataloguing-in-Publication data

Wallace, Adam, 1972- author, illustrator.
Random / Adam Wallace, author, illustrator ; Adam Laszczuk, designer.
9780987609625 (paperback)
For primary school age.
Children's stories.
Laszczuk, Adam, book designer.
A823.4

Do not stick this book in your ear.
This book is not a toy or a three course meal.

To the awesome kids in Miss Monks'
2014 Grade 3/4 class at Pembroke P.S.
Thanks heaps for being my test group!

CONTENTS

AUTHOR'S NOTE

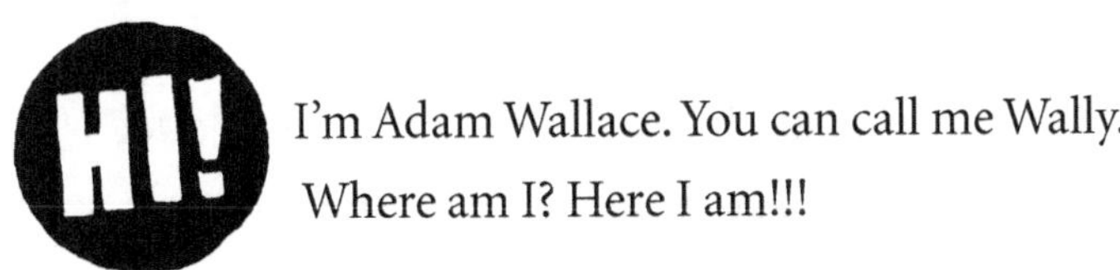

I'm Adam Wallace. You can call me Wally. Where am I? Here I am!!!

In two of my previous books, **Better Out Than In** and **Better Out Than In Number Twos**, I included an author's note, a warning if you will.

Look, to be honest, it was just me rambling on about anything that popped into my head, and now there is a whole book of this random stuff!

A WHOLE BOOK!
THIS BOOK! OMG!

Which means, 'Oh My God'. It doesn't mean, as I initially thought, 'Old Men Giggled'. And **LOL** doesn't mean 'Lots Of Love'! I found that out when someone died and I wrote to their wife and said,

"I hear that your husband died. I'm sorry. LOL."

It didn't go down too well.

Anyway, like I said, this is a book. I thought I'd let you know, because if you thought it was something to play tennis with, you would not win one single game using this book as a racquet.

No, this book is for reading, and it makes me so happy that you've chosen to read it.

It's pretty random at some points. At other points it's not random at all. Some bits are sort of random but not really.

I don't know why I said all that ... I basically just described life.

Let us continue.

Inside this book are pages, and on these pages are my thoughts. There are ramblings and ideas, lists and fears, rhymes and stories, and past and present glories.

There are notes and thoughts, bits of advice, some favourite things, and recipes with rice.

There are actually no recipes in this book that contain rice.

There are no recipes containing tofu, apples, or monkey butts either.

Oh, except for the roast monkey butt with tofu and apples.

That has all those things plus parsley.

So then.

Anyways.

I hope you enjoy reading this collection.

It was fun writing it.

TOP
FIVE
DANCE
MOVES

I like dancing. I do. Unfortunately, in a family where everyone dances, one of us had to miss out on having rhythm. It wasn't my mum, who taught ballet for 25 years. It wasn't my sister, who learnt dancing for 20 years and who danced professionally for a long time. It wasn't my dad, who learnt tap dancing. It wasn't even my nana, who was still busting a move in her 80s.

No. It was me.

But, despite the fact that I'm not a great dancer, and despite the fact that while dancing I have stepped on people, kicked people, stubbed my toe, broken a finger and broken a door, I love it! And I do have some favourite moves. What I am going to do is flick book my way through the moves. So go. Bottom right of the page. Start flicking to see my stick man bust a move!

THINGS THAT ARE BETTER LATE THAN NEVER

Pizza

(still tastes good cold!)

Anything cooked on a barbeque

(also tastes good cold)

Birthday presents

A cuddle . . . *unless it's from Aunt Beryl.*

School holidays!

$250,000,000,000 . . . *unless it's so late you're dead.*

Then it may as well be never.

LOOK AT THE SIGN.
DO NOT RUN
NOW YOU TELL ME AAAGGHHH! 
GIVE ME A HUG!
NOOOOOO!
THINGS THAT ARE NOT BETTER LATE THAN NEVER

Seeing half a worm in an apple after you've bitten into it.

Reading a use-by-date that says 1/1/1998.

Realising your pants zipper is undone. This is even worse if you realise **AFTER** you've given a presentation to a **LOT** of **EXTREMELY** important people.

Realising the toilet seat cover is down.

An airbag going off.

A birthday present from Aunt Beryl.

A cuddle from Aunt Beryl.

Pants.

MORE THINGS THAT ARE NOT BETTER LATE THAN NEVER

'LOOK OUT!' or 'DUCK!'

A PARACHUTE OPENING

TOO LATE!

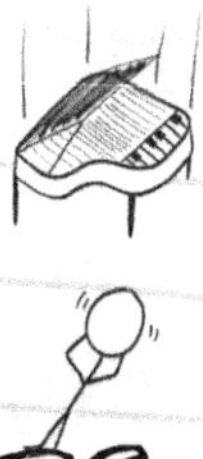

THINGS THAT ARE BETTER

NEVER!!!

Mean teachers.

A slap in the face with a wet fish.

A wet fish slapping you in the face.

A wet fish slapping you on the butt.

A wet fish slapping you on the butt with a burnt stick.

A wet stick slapping you on the fish with a burnt butt . . .

Eating all your Brussels sprouts and then finding out
that dessert is a cake Aunt Beryl made and it has
those gross fake cherries in it . . . and orange peel . . .
and all the other gross fake fruits.

Stepping in dog poo while walking.

AGGGH!
DOG POO. DIDN'T SEE IT. OH WELL, IT'LL CLEAN OFF.

Stepping in dog poo while walking in bare feet.

OH NO!!!
SHOULD HAVE WORN SHOES! OH WELL, IT'LL CLEAN OFF.

Stepping in dog poo while walking on your hands

Stepping in dog poo while walking on your tongue.

YOUR ARGUMENT HAS NO WEIGHT!
YOU'RE A BARE-FACED LIAR!
DON'T ARGUE WITH...

A shark
(unless you're on land)
NO WAY! GREAT WHITE SHARKS SUCK AT GOLF!
BITE ME.
A lion
(unless you're in the water)
BITE ME.
YOU'RE LYIN'! AS IF A LINE OF LIONS IS A PRIDE!

Jelly *(it can't speak and you will look silly)*

A baby *(they can't understand what you're saying, and halfway through the argument you will have to stop and change their nappy)*

Someone you love over something really silly

(waste of time)

A pirate *(they are too one-eyed about things and if you lose they will make you walk the plank)*

Someone who is carrying a cannon on their shoulder

(they are obviously very strong and very insane)

Someone who is already a really good arguer and who has just taken a good-arguing pill and has invented an arguing machine which increases their arguing abilities by 1,000,000% which isn't even possible but that's what it does that's how good it is and it's a Wednesday which is their peak arguing day!!!

THE
ENGLISH
LANGUAGE

When people speak to me in, say, Japanese, even though it sounds cool, I can't understand a word they're saying. So the English language is handy. I tell you what, though, there are some things about it that drive me cuckoo bonkers. Here are my questions for the English language inventors.

Why are there letter arrangements that can be said lots of different ways? Like 'o–u–g–h'. You can have 'through', 'cough', 'though', or 'thought'. So it can sound like 'ooo', 'off', 'oh', or 'or', and probably other ways as well. Someone will tell me one day that 'o–u–g–h' can be pronounced 'fizz' or something. I don't know. I just made that up and, reading it back, that was a weird thing to say. Still . . . it may happen!

Why are there words that are spelt the same but pronounced differently? Live and live. Windy and windy. Read and read. I mean, come on people! That is just nuts.

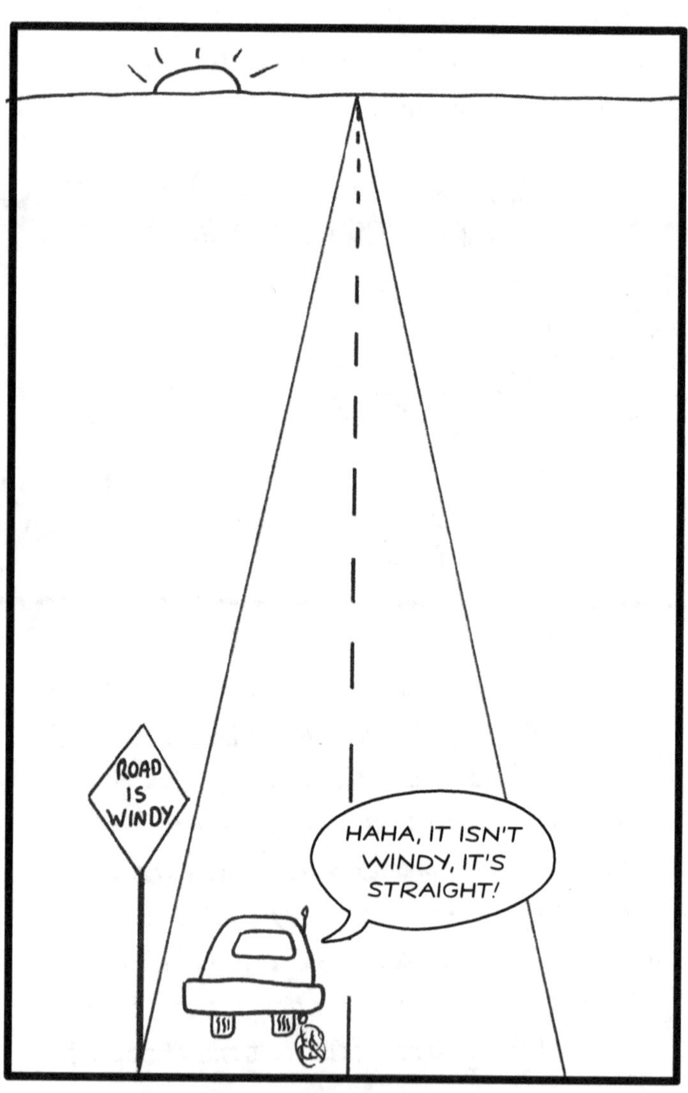

DAMN YOU, ENGLISH LANGUAGE!
ROAD IS WINDY

Why don't 'doing', 'going' and 'boing' rhyme?
In fact, does boing rhyme with anything? I don't
know. This guy gives it a go and fails dismally!

Why are some words spelt the same and sound the same,
but mean different things? 'Wee' can mean something is
little; it can mean going to the toilet; it can even mean
you're having fun as you go down a slide. 'Left' can be
a side, like your left-hand; it can mean you didn't bring
something; or it's something to do with politics.
Even 'bum' can be the bum on your body or it can be some
hobo on the street yelling stuff no—one can understand.

AAAAAAAAAGGGGGHHHHHHHHH!!!

It's confusing in so many ways!

There are other things as well, but I need to have a wee lie down to relax . . . that means a little lie down, don't be gross, Dude!!!

a Good Time

FLYING A PLANE

EATING YOUR OWN EARWAX

WORST TIME:
When you're someone who will become Prime Minister of Australia . . . for a little while . . . and then not . . . and then again . . . and then not . . . actually, it's ALWAYS the worst time! DON'T EAT EARWAX!
HMMM, THIS EAR WAX ISN'T BAD. NOT AS NICE AS MINE THOUGH. NEEDS MORE SNOT IN IT.

SLEEPING

GOOD TIME: When you're tucked up in bed

BAD TIME: When your teacher's telling you off
ARE YOU ASLEEP? THAT'S 1,000,000,000 YEARS OF DETENTION!!!

WORST TIME: No explanation necessary

DOING HANDSTANDS

A.B.
I HATE YOU,
AUNT BERYL.

GROSSNESS

I don't get grossed out. It's one of the random things about me. Actually, when people try and gross me out, what usually happens is I start to feel a bit hungry.

Go figure that out!

Anyway. This section's about gross stuff, so I hope you can handle it. **ENJOY!**

For example, let's say you're at someone's house where everything is perfectly perfect.

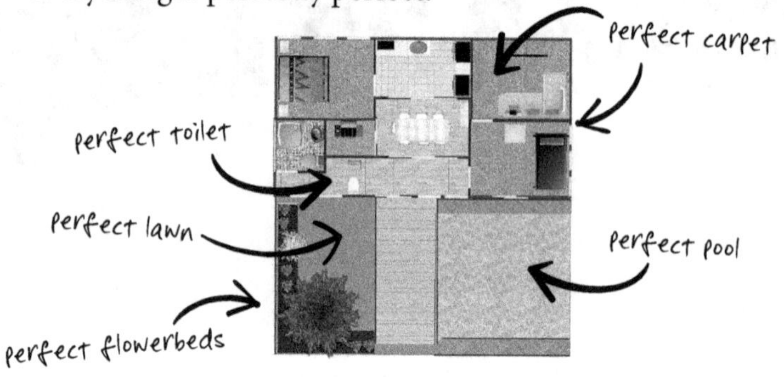

There are expensive and perfect paintings on the walls. There are loads of perfect things you can't touch. Even the poodle has a little poo bag nappy so that it doesn't soil the perfect grass on the perfect lawn. The owners also believe that children should be seen and not heard.

You try and hold it in.

But you can't.

They serve you sooooo much perfect food. You are so full, and when you politely drink some of the fizzy stuff they give you, you need to burp. You try to ask if you can be excused, You don't get the words out. Instead, you burp. A teeny, tiny little burp. You laugh and apologise.

But then it happens.

That teeny, tiny burp loosens everything. All that perfect food and perfect drink forces its way up from deep in your belly and . . . you spew. Everywhere. You spew on the perfectly set table, on the perfect carpet and walls, and some of it even splatters on the paintings. Your host has a weak stomach, and the smell and sight of you spewing makes her spew. She spews on the dog and the couch. Then the dog eats it. It's so gross that you need to spew again, so you run outside. You run over their perfect grass. Your eyes are watering from all the spew, and you accidentally run over the perfect flowerbed, squashing the perfect flowers before spewing in the perfect swimming pool.

See? How funny would that be?

Here's a picture of it . . .
we had to censor it
because it was too
gross, but you
get the idea.

THEY SAY: "I would never pass wind in a public place.
That is disgusting."

THEY MEAN: "I fart all the time, but I have somehow
worked out how to angle my butt cheeks so the
pop-offs are silent. Then, if it's a pongy stinker,
I blame the dog. If there's no dog,
I blame the baby. If there's no baby,
I blame the nearest person
I don't like."

THEY SAY: "Some people believe burps are a sign
of appreciation of good food. I believe burps are simply
rude and vulgar."

THEY MEAN: "I wish I could burp the alphabet,
but because the burps I do are so weak and wussy
I will pretend that I think burps are rude. Really I'm
just jealous because I know I would always come last
in a burping contest."

 "I would never pick my nose."

 "I would never pick my nose if I thought someone could catch me. So I do it in my car at the lights, and thank god for those magic windows the car salesman told me about that are darker when the car's stopped. I also do it when I'm teaching a class and all the students are looking at their work. I do it in the cinema. I do it when I'm in bed at night, and if I don't have a hanky I just wipe it on the underneath of my pillow. I would never eat it though. Unless I had to, like if there was nowhere to wipe it or I was starving in a desert and there was nothing else to eat except live scorpions and ear wax."

 "Girls don't fart."

 "Girls are already stinky without need-ing to fart. If they farted then they would stink so bad the world would explode."

I apologise to all the girls who read that last bit and got offended. I don't actually think girls are stinky. James Smitty told me it would be funny to put it in. Besides, it's crazy to think that if someone farted the world would explode … unless it was James Smitty. Oh man, one time he farted in Western Australia and the world didn't explode, but I reckon it may have got a few cracks in it.

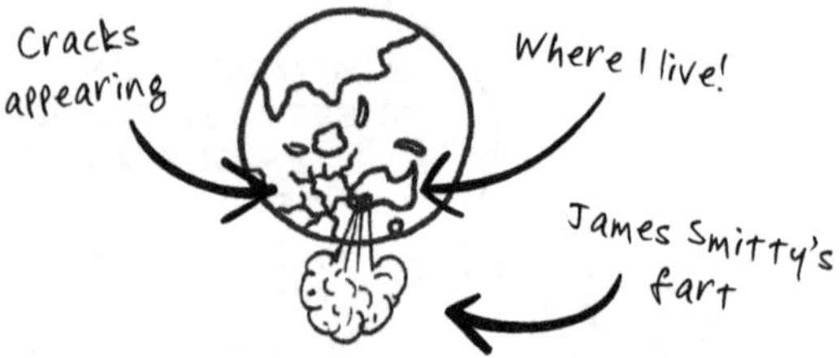

So I'm sorry if any girls got offended. And anyway, like I said, I know it's not true. I know girls do fart, because one time I was on a train and this lady sitting next to me let off a silent but deadly, and it totally stunk to high heaven. She blamed the baby, but I just said, "Give up, Mum, I know it was you."

FRIES

So. You know how at a certain fast food place (not naming any names . . . McDONALDS!), when you order some food they're like, "Would you like fries with that?"

What I want to do is go in and have things play out a little like this . . .

THEM: "Good afternoon Sir, how may I help you?"

ME: "I'll have nothing thanks."

THEM: "Yes, Sir. Would you like fries with that?"

ME: "Yep, regular please."

THEM: "Excellent Sir, anything else?"

ME: "No thanks."

Then they would say how much it costs, I would get my fries and a whole burst of fun.

But I haven't been brave enough to go in and ask for nothing yet.

One day I'll do it.

Seriously.

I WILL.

DOGS
(PART ONE)

I looooooooooooove dogs. They are the best pet ever.
Cats are not. Cats are snobs who sleep lots and want
you to work for them. Dogs rule. You can walk dogs,
wrestle with dogs, run with dogs, throw balls for dogs,
get licked on the face by dogs . . . okay, so that isn't so
great, especially if your dog just licked its own butt.

Dogs are always happy to see you, too. Cats sort of
turn and partly acknowledge you have walked in the
door, but that's it. Dogs almost knock you flying they
get so excited.

There are, however, some things about dogs
I must pass on.

1. If a dog is frothing at the mouth, growling, snarling, and barking, run away screaming. Do not, I repeat, do not try to scratch its tummy. This dog has rabies and will kill you. Even worse, it will get frothy slobber all over you.

2. If you're pretending to sniff your dog's butt to make it feel happy, make sure your sister isn't there taking a photo or video.

3. If you want to seem tough, do not, I repeat, do not get a poodle, a Pomeranian, or a Shih Tzu, even if the name sounds funny and a little bit rude. To appear tough you need a dog that doesn't look like it has just come from the beauty salon.

4. It really, really sucks when your dog dies, but if you remember all the awesome, fun times you had with him or her, that dog will never really leave you. R.I.P. Krueger.

WEEEEEEEE!
HAHAHA! YOU CAN'T SEE ME!

TOP FIVE
SUPER POWERS
STOP FLEXING AND HELP ME!
I'M SO STRONG!

SUPER STRENGTH

Super strength is awesome because you would always win fights with your step-brother and he wouldn't get the chance to fart in your face and make you cry like a little baby . . . or at least, that's what I've heard . . .

INVISIBILITY

Invisibility rocks! You could sneak away when you get into trouble! My dog used to shut her eyes when she was in trouble. She thought if she couldn't see us, we couldn't see her. It didn't work.

Apart from being awesome, imagine how much you would save on airfares if you could fly!!!

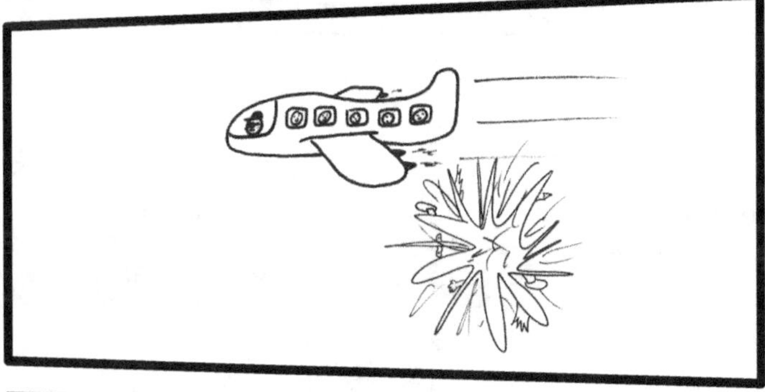

Okay, so for starters you would be able to see if your toast was cooked without having to pop it up . . . of course, a see-through toaster would do this too. Hey, that would be cool!

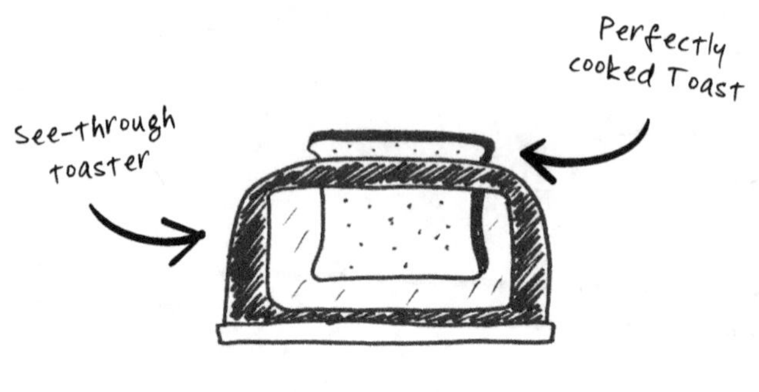

5. BEING ABLE TO EXPLODE YOUR HEAD

Imagine how cool this would be! Say, for example, someone says they'll tell you a story that will blow your mind. You could listen politely and then, after the final line, make your head explode. Observe . . .

BIG WORDS

BLAH BLAH BLAH
BLAH BLAH BLAH
BLAH BLAH!

BLAH BLAH BL
BLAH BLAH BL
BLAH BLAH.

It used to drive me crazy when people used big words. I would be somewhere, and someone would say something like, "There's a lot of susurration in the crowd."

I would turn to the person next to me and be like, "What does susurration mean?" And they would be like, "It means whispering or rustling." And I would be like (without susurration),

"WELL WHY DON'T THEY JUST SAY WHISPERING OR RUSTLING?"

Now though, I think big words are funny, and here are some of the funniest big words I know. Use them if you want to. It would totally confuse your mum if you said something like:

In fact, it would confuse her so much that this might happen . . .

Of course, this is not an accurate picture of what would happen. Your mum will definitely be wearing different earrings to the ones in the picture.

Gobbledygook – nonsense

Puggle – a baby echidna

Goatsucker – common name for nocturnal birds such as the frogmouth, nightjar and whippoorwill (Awesome! Even the names of the birds in the definition are funny!)

Spiflicate – to destroy

Slubberdegullion – a worthless fellow

Muckle – a large amount

Pandiculate – to stretch and yawn

Sloom – to sleep soundly

THINGS THAT LOOK CUTE BUT WILL SCRATCH YOUR EYES OUT IF YOU TRY AND HUG THEM

HUG?

AAGGHH!
MY EYE
EAR OW!

AWWWWW! TOO CUTE! GIVE US A HUG, LITTLE FELLA!

OMG! YOU'RE LIKE A NINJA! HEY, WHERE ARE MY EYEBALLS?

YOU ARE SOOOO KUTE. KOME ON. GIVE ME A KUDDLE.

AAAGGGGHHH!!! DAMN YOU, ENGLISH LANGUAGE!

COME ON THEN. LAY ONE ON ME!

I SERIOUSLY HATE YOU, AUNT BERYL.

HUG ME, YOU CUTE LITTLE HOBO!

AWWWW! I LOVE HUGS! THANK YOU!!!

HOBO ATAK!
AGGGGHHHH, MY EYEBALLS! THIS CRAZY OLD HOBO IS CRAZY!

ENEMIES

Enemies are mean. It's true. And they usually want to kill you or cause you pain. You virtually never get someone who says they're your mortal enemy but who then brings you a homemade chocolate cake, topped with the words 'I love you' written in pink icing (Although I am allergic to dairy and can't have sugar either, so that actually is something an enemy might do to me! Those monsters!).

Enemies usually have stupid reasons for being your enemy.
Yep, it may be that one day you got a question right in school when they knew the answer and wanted to say it. It may be you come from a different part of town, or another country. It may be you get better sandwiches than them for lunch. It may be you're faster than them and always beat them in running races. It may be that they asked you to help them one time and you said, "Get lost, loser, I wouldn't help you if it was helping

day and we lived on Planet Helpful and I was the most helpful person who lived there and I had been put in a **MAKE-YOU-HELPFUL-MACHINE**™ turned on full."

Oh. Okay. That last bit actually *is* a pretty good reason for someone to be your enemy, and you're really mean for saying that! You should go and apologise and hope they haven't invented a **MAKE-YOU-TEENY-TINY RAY GUN**™ or something.

**Enemies can turn into evil scientists
that want to rule the world.** So it might be
good to try and make up with them quickly. If they
do end up ruling the world, you want to be on their
side. Otherwise you may end up digging poo holes
for the giant killer mutant ants they've created to
be their monster army of giant killer mutant ants.

Enemies often have quite large heads.
I don't know why this happens, but it's true. Huge
heads. I only tell you this in case you want to buy
them a hat as a peace offering. It's probably a good
idea to go for an XXL size so that it fits on their
giant noggin.

MWAAWAHAHAHAHA . . .
UH OH. LOSING BALANCE.
BRAIN TOO HEAVY.

WHUP WHUP WHUP
WHUP WHUP! I'M
GOING DOWN!

STUPID
GIANT GENIUS
BRAIN.

SMELLS THAT ARE GOOD

Musk Lifesavers

Any other berry

Strawberry and Cream lollies

Peppermint

Cut grass

Cinnamon

Bubble gum, especially grape flavour

Coconut

Bread and butter pudding when it's baking . . . mmmmmmm, bread and butter pudding baking

SMELLS
THAT
ARE
BAD

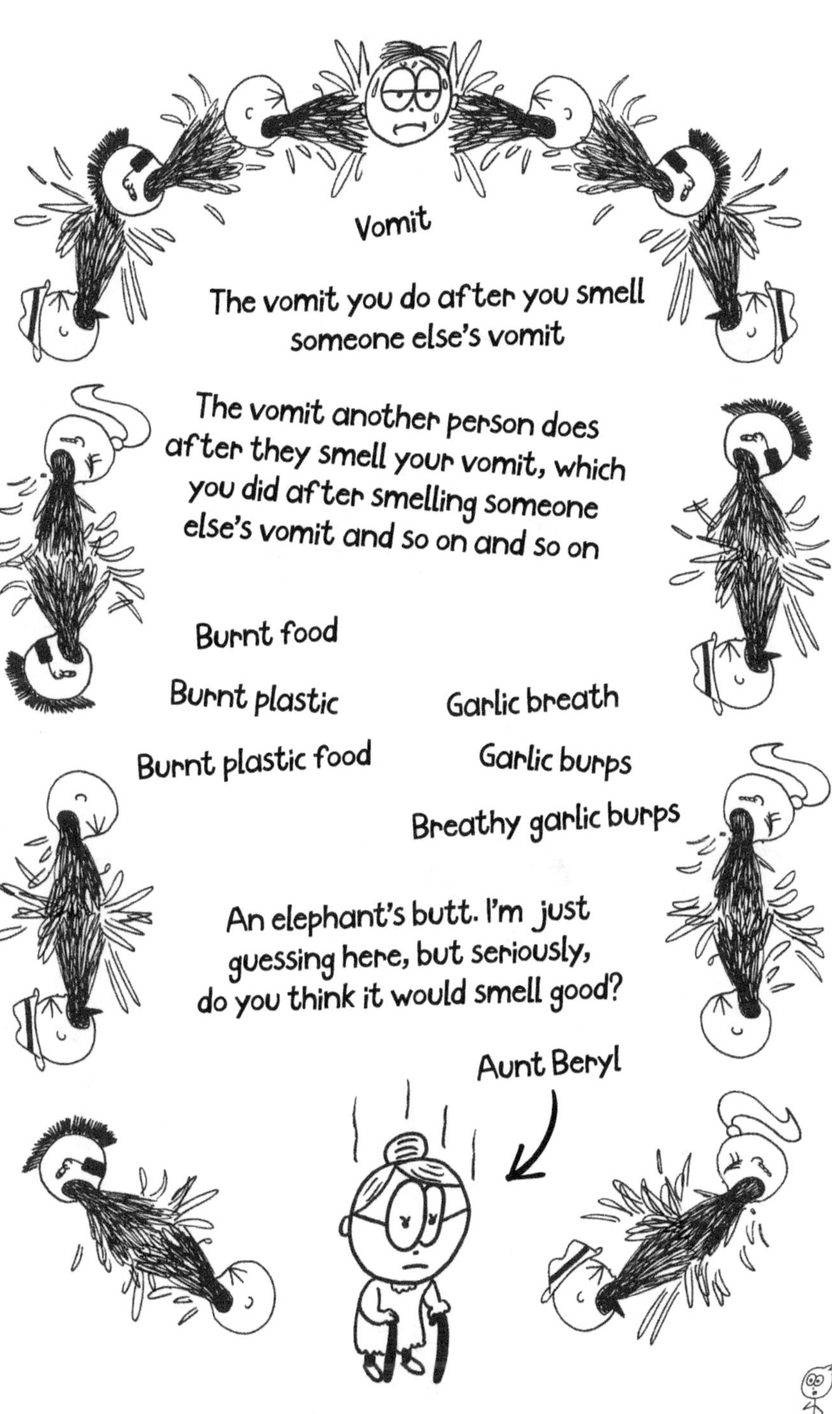

Vomit

The vomit you do after you smell
someone else's vomit

The vomit another person does
after they smell your vomit, which
you did after smelling someone
else's vomit and so on and so on

Burnt food

Burnt plastic

Burnt plastic food

Garlic breath

Garlic burps

Breathy garlic burps

An elephant's butt. I'm just
guessing here, but seriously,
do you think it would smell good?

Aunt Beryl

GO TO
WWW.RANDOMWALLY.COM
TO SEE A VIDEO OF ME
SMELLING GROSS
STUFF.

LIVING IN OUTER SPACE

Why are people so keen to explore outer space? Why do I always hear talk about how it would be great to set up a colony on the moon, or Mars, or wherever? Seriously. I have seen photos of those places. I've seen the movies. Why on earth (hehe) would you ever want to live on the moon or Mars or Uranus? I certainly wouldn't want to live on Uranus.

The only good thing about living on the moon is that you would be able to take those giant slow-motion steps … and that's it! Unless it was like on a TV show and there was a little alien that became my friend and got me in and out of trouble. Actually, that usually happens if the alien comes to earth.

If I was on their planet they would probably just take me to their leader, use all kinds of weird probes on me and end up chopping me to pieces for research …

. . . and that would pretty much suck, and is another reason why I don't want to live on the moon.

Tell me something good about living on the moon and why it would be better than living on earth. I am willing to be convinced, but I don't reckon anyone will actually be able to do it.

Go on then. Email me. Send all your reasons why living on the moon would be better than living on earth to randomwally@hotmail.com and see if you can convince me to live on the moon.

Good luck, I say, good luck to you all!

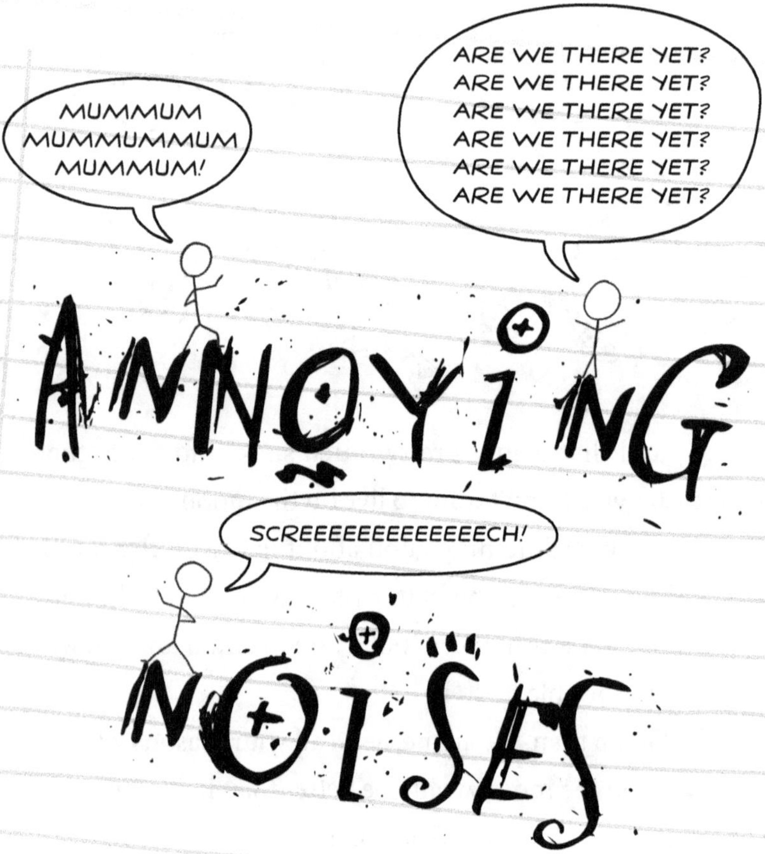

ANNOYING NOISES

The mating call of the West Amazonian Flesh–Eating Bug.

Possums screeching . . . the actual sound isn't annoying, but it annoys me. They look so cute but sound like they're vampire zombies.

Sniffing/snorting/hucking up a gorbie

Crunchy chewing of food

Aunt Beryl singing

TOP
FiVE
FAVOURITE
FOODS

1. Spaghetti Bolognese or fettuccine Bolognese, or gnocchi Bolognese, or ravioli with Bolognese, or rice with Bolognese, or, best of all, Chicken Schnitzel with Bolognese sauce on top.

2. Chicken Schnitzel and gravy

3. Roast dinner and gravy

4. Chips and gravy

5. Fried rice and gravy . . . okay, look, pretty much anything with gravy. Why?

BECAUSE GRAVY MAKES IT GOOD!!!

DOGS
(PART TWO)

THINGS DOGS DO THAT WE SHOULD DO

Try 100% all the time

Play a lot

Always be joyful

Be loyal

Be happy to see people you love

Stay clear of crazy evil vampire zombie dogs

Sniff someone's butt

Lick someone's face

Eat our own or somebody else's vomit

ROAST MONKEY BUTT WITH TOFU AND APPLES

INGREDIENTS

One monkey butt, both cheeks
Ten apples, sliced
300g tofu, sliced
Parsley, chopped

METHOD

1. Pre-heat oven to 180 degrees Celsius.
2. Place monkey butt in front of your face and pretend it can talk.
3. Grease baking tray.
4. Grease lightning.
5. Place monkey butt in baking tray.
6. Place slices of apple around monkey butt.
7. Make fart sound, blame monkey butt.
8. Place tofu slices so they are sticking upright out of monkey butt.
9. Place baking tray in oven.
10. Say, "Please don't cook me" in a monkey voice.
11. Cook monkey butt for 100 minutes or until butt is brown.
12. Sprinkle parsley on top.
13. Serve with vegetables and gravy.

MONKEY BUTT
COOKBOOK
TASTY MONKEY BUTTS FOR EVERYONE!
EXCEPT ME!
MONKEY BUTT COOKBOOK

DOCTORS AND LOLLIPOPS

I finally worked it out. I always wondered why doctors gave you a lollipop — or some other sort of lolly — after you had an appointment. I had always thought it was because they felt a bit sorry for sticking a thermometer up your butt (They don't do that anymore. It goes under your tongue or arm or in your ear, and hopefully it's been cleaned since it was up someone's butt).

Anyway.

I have come to realise it is all a big conspiracy. The doctors and the dentists are all in it together. They are like some big old evil gang of evil evilness. Here's how it works. I've used a flowchart to explain.

Okay, so you'll have to turn the page for the next bit . . .

The bit after this I mean . . .

Turn the page . . .

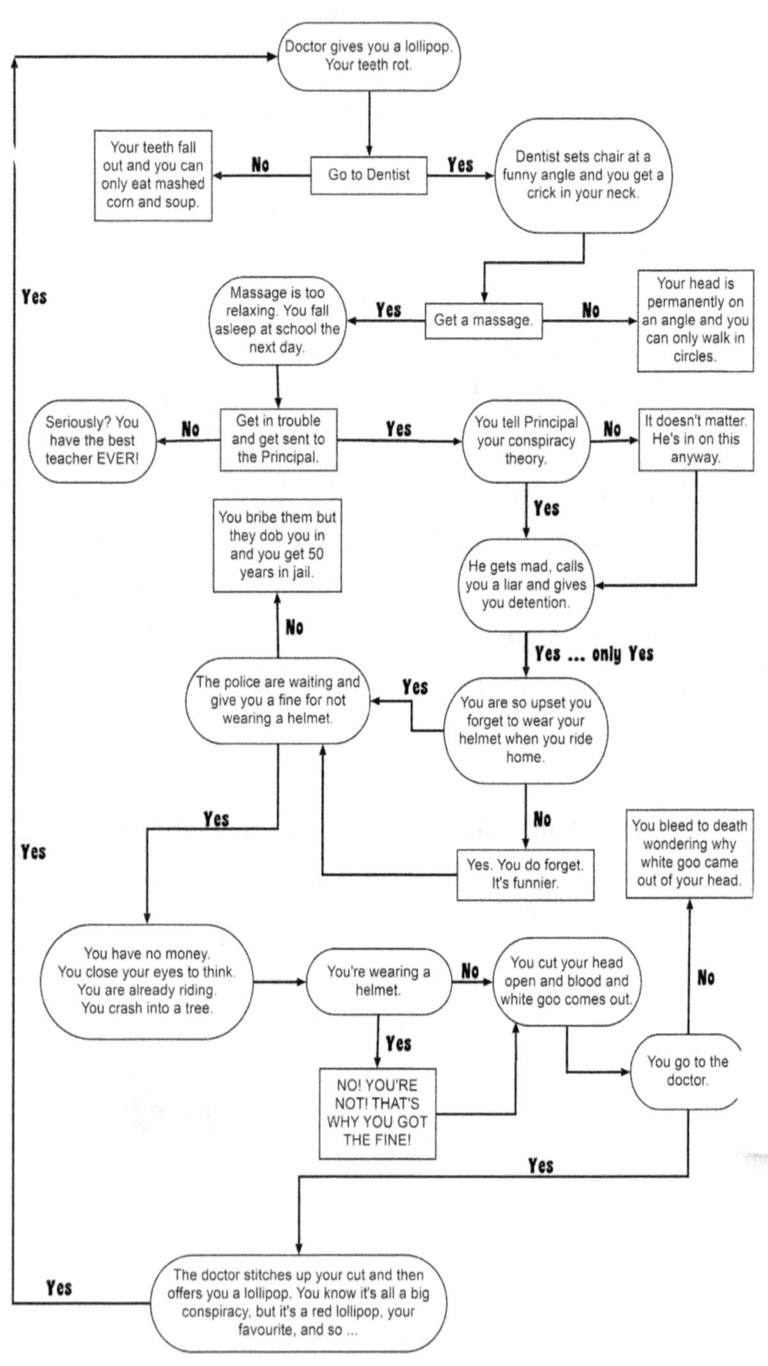

Doctor gives you a lollipop. Your teeth rot.
Your teeth fall out and you can only eat mashed corn and soup.
No
Go to Dentist
Yes
Dentist sets chair at a funny angle and you get a crick in your neck.
Massage is too relaxing. You fall asleep at school the next day.
Yes
Get a massage.
No
Your head is permanently on an angle and you can only walk in circles.
Seriously? You have the best teacher EVER!
No
Get in trouble and get sent to the Principal.
Yes
You tell Principal your conspiracy theory.
No
It doesn't matter. He's in on this anyway.
Yes
You bribe them but they dob you in and you get 50 years in jail.
He gets mad, calls you a liar and gives you detention.
Yes ... only Yes
The police are waiting and give you a fine for not wearing a helmet.
No
Yes
You are so upset you forget to wear your helmet when you ride home.
No
Yes
You bleed to death wondering why white goo came out of your head.
Yes
Yes. You do forget. It's funnier.
You have no money. You close your eyes to think. You are already riding. You crash into a tree.
You're wearing a helmet.
No
You cut your head open and blood and white goo comes out.
No
Yes
NO! YOU'RE NOT! THAT'S WHY YOU GOT THE FINE!
You go to the doctor.
Yes
Yes
The doctor stitches up your cut and then offers you a lollipop. You know it's all a big conspiracy, but it's a red lollipop, your favourite, and so ...

BAD DREAMS

I have pretty bad dreams … I mean, not bad enough that I need a plastic cover over my mattress any more or anything, but they are pretty bad.

I've written a little poem about it.

Here it is.

Read it.

I dreamt that I turned up
naked to school,

I dreamt that everyone
called me a fool.

I dreamt my parents told me I was adopted,

dreamt I almost took the winning catch . . .
but I dropped it!

I dreamt a giant spider
was on my face,

I dreamt I was in a beauty
contest . . . I got last place!

I dreamt I was boxing the
heavyweight champ,

I dreamt I was electrocuted by my bedside lamp.

I dreamt there was a monster
under my bed,
I dreamt I was in a coffin . . .
but I wasn't dead!

I dreamt I could fly, because I was a fly,

I dreamt I poked a toothbrush into my eye.

So my dreams are pretty bad, it has to be said,
In fact, maybe I need that plastic sheet back on my bed.

PORTMANTEAUS

I looooove portmanteaus (You say it 'port-man-toes'!). This is when you put two words together to make a new word. For example, if you put together 'cool' and 'bananas' (like when you say 'cool bananas' for something good), you may end up with 'coonanas'! Here are some portmanteaus that I made up.

Smappy – This merges 'smiling' and 'happy' together, and means you are really happy. I like to imagine Jim Carrey as The Mask saying this. If you don't know who or what The Mask is, go and watch it **NOW!** Anyway, he would say it like this:

Grousome – This is 'grouse' and 'awesome' together, and means something is really, really great! In a sentence? "That was so grousome."

Rucks – a mixture of 'really' and 'sucks'. It makes you sound like Scooby Doo, but that's okay. In a sentence? "This maths test rucks!"

Frits – okay, so this is a few words together, 'frightened out of my wits'. In a sentence? "I am so frits right now!" Or, "I was totally frits watching that movie!"

Grogusting – a mixture of 'gross' and 'disgusting'. In a sentence? "Mum, these Brussels sprouts are grogusting!"

Gorillagon – A 'gorilla' mixed with a 'dragon'. Possibly the toughest animal ever. It would also make (and eat!) tasty fried banana fritters.

Now go and make up your own! As many as you can! It's awesome fun.

TRYING TO SLEEP

Here are some things that do, or may possibly, keep me awake at night. You can try and pick which ones have actually happened.

Having a song going round and round in my head over and over and over again.

Being worried about something.

Thunderstorms

Possums jumping on the roof.

Possums jumping on my face.

A giant spider jumping on my face.

My wife talking in her sleep.

My wife snoring in her sleep.

My wife burping in her sleep.

My wife dreaming about giving a
massage and massaging me in the face.

My wife dreaming about being a boxer
and punching me in the face.

My wife dreaming about being
a crazy psycho chainsaw killer
and wanting to chainsaw off my face.

BEING GROWN UP

 It had to happen. I had to eventually talk about what it means to be grown up. I get called immature a lot. I also get told to act my age, act like an adult, blah blahdy blah blah yah sucks boo to you.

You know what I reckon? Do you **really** want to know what I think? I hope you do, because this is the last section in the whole book. You've read the rest of it (**I hope**), so it would be crazy to stop here with just one section to go. If you did that, I would have to come around and give you a noogie. Don't know what a noogie is? Let's just say . . . no, I won't give it away, that is your new research project.

(www.merriam-webster.com/dictionary/noogie might help you out . . .)

Anyway, being grown up . . . all those snooty bums who sit with their noses in the air, saying boring snooty blah blah things like, "Gosh, look at that man, he's acting like a child. Yes, he does seem to be enjoying himself, but he should show some restraint and act like a proper adult," I reckon **they** are the ones who haven't grown up and who aren't mature.

In the dictionary, it says mature means ripe . . . why would you want to be ripe too soon? Do you know what happens to fruit after it's ripe? That's right, it starts

going off! It goes all rotten and stinky and wrinkly and gross, just like Aunt Beryl.

I think you mature over your whole life. It's a process. I think maturity is being totally **comfortable** with who you are. It's being **responsible** for your own actions. It's knowing your **strengths**, and it's knowing the things that bring you the greatest **joy**. It's **caring for** and **respecting** other people and letting them **honestly express** who they are, without trying to drag them down or make them be people they're not.

It's being the person **you** dream of being, and not pretending to be someone else to make other people happy.

It's living life to its fullest, going for your dreams, being led by joy but working hard, and it's about finding fun in everything you do, as long as all of that means you don't hurt other people.

And if that means that you might jump around and play and act silly to entertain a toddler; or if that means you stop blaming other people and complaining; or if that means you try something even if it means you might fail; or if that means you will do **anything** to make your dreams come true, even when other people say you're wasting your time; if you are fully in the moment and loving being who you are, then that, in my view, is being grown up  mature.

So to all those people who still think that to be grown up you need to be boring, I say, "Yah sucks boo to you, you snooty bums. If that's what **you** want to do, that's fine, but don't expect me to be a boring old fart who lies on their death bed wishing they'd had more fun and lived their life a little."

When **I'm** on my death bed I want to be tired from living such an awesome life. I'll be ripe and mature, and all I'll be wishing for is for the nurses to turn on the death bed electric blanket because it's cold, and my hip is sore from when I fell over and broke it dancing at Aunt Beryl's 101st birthday party.

So that's the lesson from this book. I'm being serious now, this is the lesson for self-improvement that I've learned and want to pass on to you. Take from it what you want, and chuck out the rest. But here it is. Live your life. **Really** live it. Be yourself; be real; take responsibility;

care for other people; follow your heart and be led by joy; go for your dreams; **always** look at how you can make something fun and exciting; **always** work hard and **always** give 100%. Then, once you find out your strengths, how you can help the world, and what truly gives you joy, follow those feelings. That is when you'll be at your happiest.

Stay gold, everyone.

I'll see you at the monkeys.

Wally.

ABOUT THE AUTHOR

1.

Adam Wallace, sitting in a tree,
D-R-A-W-I-N-G
Writes the books, draws the pics,
Scratches his head if someone says, "NITS!"

2.

Adam Wallace, he writes lots of books,
Grew up, on a farm, with a lot of chooks.
They laid eggs, they did poo,
Nasty ones ended up in a stew.
Adam Wallace, he writes lots of books,
But he no longer has any chooks.

3.

Adam Wallace, was an engineer,
But it bored him to tears, I fear.
So he wrote, a children's book,
When he was little he was a sooky sook.
Adam Wallace's friends are engineers,
He looks like an elf with his pointy ears.